THiS BOOK iS FOR

- You want to become more self-aware;

- You want to feel good about yourself;

- You love life and want more of it;

- You want to release your worry habit;

- You are ready to be more positive;

- You want to reduce your anger levels;

- You want to feel healthier and happier;

- You want to feel more content and grounded;

- You want to recover or sustain your MoJo.

WHAT PEOPLE ARE SAYING...

You can tell immediately when someone walks into the office on a Monday if they've got their MoJo or not - and if not, steer well clear!

For many, the thought of returning to work on a Monday is a real MoJo killer. All the stress of the previous week comes flooding back and brings a feeling of dread. No wonder it is the worst day for absenteeism.

Scientist Ann McCracken is an authority on the topics of stress, well-being and resilience, and believes she has found a way to get your MoJo back on Monday morning, or indeed any other day of the week.

In this inventive new book, *How to get back your MoJo*, she brings her scientific and medical research background to simplify recent leaps in knowledge of Neuroscience which have clarified the mind-body connection.

Ann suggests we all have an inner Gremlin which feeds on our emotions and this then directs our behaviour. The controversial aspect of the concept is YOU can choose what emotions you give your Gremlin to eat, resulting in stress/ill health or feeling GREAT and recovering your MoJo/feel-good factor.

Positive emotions like delight, excitement and empathy create MoJo and good health, whereas unhelpful emotions like anger, despair and helplessness create passive and out of control feelings.

This book presents a unique way to consider taking control of your reactions and your health.

ABOUT THE AUTHOR

Ann McCracken is an authority on the topics of stress, well-being and resilience. She uses her background in scientific and medical research to simplify recent leaps in neuroscience knowledge which have clarified the mind-body connection.

Ann carried out postgraduate research relating to rheumatoid arthritis. She held scientific managerial posts; in one post, she directed research to measure antibiotic residues in meat and fish, and in another, she and her team monitored the development of antibiotic resistance. She advised local GPs and consultants on microbiological findings.

Ann lived in Dubai for two years where she enjoyed exploring a different culture and had the opportunity to teach music to pre-school and schoolchildren.

On returning to the UK, Ann's scientific experience was channelled into teaching biology, working with young people aged 11 to 18. This honed her training skills and 10 years later she launched her private practice after training as a Stress Management Practitioner, Hypnotherapist and NLP Practitioner.

Since then, Ann has worked with more than 2,000 clients, adding further skills to her already extensive repertoire: Reiki 2, Emotional Freedom Technique (EFT), Eye Movement Desensitising and Reprogramming (EMDR), CBT, Management and Emotional Intelligence Coaching.

In conjunction with her private practice, Ann was Director of AMC2, a company focused on management training on how to avoid stress and achieve well-being and resilience. She has worked with PLCs, SMEs and Public Sector organisations for the past 18 years.

With her colleague, Jenny Edwards, Ann wrote an ISMA[UK] accredited e-learning programme on stress, well-being and resilience which now resides on www.e-careers.com.

As Chair of the International Management Association in the UK (ISMA[UK]) from 2004 to 2008, Ann regularly gave radio interviews to local and national networks and wrote copy for magazines. She was interviewed by Jenni Murray about stress for the Radio 4's *Woman's Hour*.

Since 2003, Ann has developed her keynote speaker profile at conferences throughout the UK and India on a wide variety of topics, including her beloved Gremlins.

She's used the 'Gremlin' concept to explain how people can regain their MoJo because it clarifies the concept of self-responsibility.

A GiFT FOR YOU!

To help you to get the most out of this book,
I have created a companion eBook of additional
tools, tips, strategies and exercises.
This is complimentary and my gift to you.

To download it, and to stay up to date with
additional case studies and insights, visit
www.annmccracken.co.uk

DO YOU GET THAT MONDAY MORNING
FEELING - ALL WEEK?

HOW TO GET BACK YOUR MOJO

WOW!

BY UNDERSTANDING YOUR INNER GREMLIN

ANN McCRACKEN

Published by Filament Publishing Ltd
16 Croydon Road, Beddington, Croydon,
Surrey, CRO 4PA, United Kingdom.
Telephone: +44(0)20 8688 2598
www.filamentpublishing.com

© 2017 Ann McCracken
ISBN 978-1-911425-06-9

The right of Ann McCracken to be identified
as the author of this work has been asserted
by her in accordance with the
Designs and Copyrights Act 1988.

CONTENTS

Dedication

This book is dedicated to the inspirational, late Professor Candace B. Pert, neuroscientist and innovative thinker, and to my patient, and understanding husband Andrew, whose encouragement and support has been motivational.

I would like to thank Chris Day from Filament Publishing for recognising the potential of the Health Gremlin concept and for the fun and laughs we've had on the way. His knowledge and expertise is truly amazing.

I would also like to acknowledge the brilliant expertise of cartoonist Clive Francis who has brought the 'Gremlins' to life
www.cliveportfolio.com

CHAPTER 1:

YOUR SELF-AWARENESS ADVENTURE

**"Your vision will become clear only when
you can look into your own heart.
Who looks outside, dreams;
who looks inside, awakes."
Carl G. Jung**

Self-awareness is the conscious knowledge of your own character; your feelings, motives, and desires. It is about knowing your own strengths and limitations, understanding your own emotions and the impact of your behaviour on yourself and others in diverse situations.

The more you know about yourself, the better you are at adapting to life changes, especially those which have the potential to sabotage your personal plans.

The great psychoanalyst, Sigmund Freud, wrote much about the relevance of emotions. He championed the belief that the more you pay attention to your emotions and how you tick, the better you'll understand yourself and why you do the things you do.

You do not need to undergo years of psychoanalysis to know and observe yourself. Knowing and noticing can help you appreciate your learned biases and assumptions, which can make you very judgemental or very tolerant of a situation or person.

Our body is in constant flux. It is reacting and responding, adapting and learning. Depending on your outlook, this could be exciting or scary!

A balanced mind and body is healthy, vibrant, content and grounded. It feels comfortable and relaxed. It is like a boat gently but steadily moving through calm waters with the occasional wave or two to navigate. This does not mean life is dull or tedious; it is more likely to be serene and joyful, playful and fun-loving.

When you are emotionally balanced, you are an efficient, effective individual, employee, manager, director or chairman. When you are emotionally balanced, you are coping well with life's challenges and stress is not an issue. People whose emotions are balanced can be buzzing and enthusiastic as well as thoughtful and calm. This means that they can express their emotions comfortably, not outrageously. They do not suppress emotions for a long time, but express their feelings, opening them up for discussion and negotiation. Emotionally balanced discussion brings the opportunity to resolve issues.

There are many other aspects of self-awareness. You may know your Intelligence Quotient (IQ), a subjective measure of intellect which requires the ability to read fluently and apply your knowledge in a given period of time.

However, if you are dyslexic (you find reading/comprehension challenging), while it may be useful to get a measure of your IQ, it certainly won't give you the whole picture.

There are many well-known individuals who were/are dyslexic:

- Pablo Picasso, artist
- Tom Cruise, actor
- Richard Branson, businessman and entrepreneur
- Bill Gates, Microsoft boss
- Steven Spielberg, director
- Mohammed Ali, World Heavyweight Champion boxer
- Duncan Goodhew, Olympic gold medal-winning swimmer
- Magic Johnson, basketball star
- Diamond Dallas Page, World Wrestling Champion
- Steve Redgrave, rower and Olympic gold medalist

IQ can be a useful measure at some level, but it isn't the last word on a person's abilities, as evidenced in the previous list.

I've had personal experience of individuals with dyslexia and their understandable emotions of frustration, anxiety and anger. It can take some time for their IQ to show itself; their skills need understanding and encouragement if they are to be developed. The previous list of people is only a fraction of the amazing people who have triumphed over such a challenge.

Self-awareness is an important aspect of Emotional Intelligence (EQ), which may be even more important than IQ!

Emotional Intelligence is described as the capacity to be aware of, control, and express your emotions, as well as the ability to recognise, understand and influence the emotions of others.

In his 1996 book *Emotional Intelligence: Why it can matter more than IQ*, Daniel Goleman explained that people with high self-awareness are: "...aware of their moods as they are having them." This touches on the concept of mindfulness which involves focusing on the present moment – and noticing how you're feeling and what you are thinking/doing/hearing.

Relying on the outside world for inner happiness just does not work. Happiness happens when we let go of ourselves at the deepest, innermost level rather than trying to change our world outside. This is what happens when you release your MoJo – that special charm of attraction which comes from just being your true charismatic self.

Self-confidence is another area of self-awareness. It means having a strong sense of your own self-worth and not relying on others for your validation of yourself.

People with self-confidence are charismatic, assertive and comfortable with their own opinions and don't feel the need to foist them onto others. They can get their point across without upsetting other people or becoming upset themselves. And they actively learn from their mistakes too... It pays to be self-confident! There are many issues in the twenty-first century which challenge our self-confidence, particularly the high prevalence of addictions. For example, people are becoming increasingly addicted to technology, gambling, drugs, food (especially sugar), alcohol, and sex. But in a consumer society like ours, is it any wonder that addiction is such a growing menace?

In the following chapters, we will explore some of these aspects of self-awareness from the viewpoint of how human beings' behaviours affect their Personal Health Gremlin.

CHAPTER 2:

INTRODUCING THE HEALTH GREMLINS

You may have noticed some unusual illustrations in the last chapter... Those odd little creatures are the Health Gremlins and it's time I introduced them more formally...

In this book, a Gremlin relates to our personal health and its behaviour depends on how we feed it!

Historical Gremlins

Gremlins are usually thought of as mischievous creatures and that makes sense when you look at the possible derivation of the name from the Old English word 'gremain' which means 'vexing'. By the middle of the twentieth century gremlins had acquired a reputation for being mechanically oriented, with a specific interest in aircraft.

Author Roald Dahl is credited with making gremlins famous around the world with his first children's novel *The Gremlins*. These creatures, which looked like tiny men and women, lived on RAF fighters with their families.

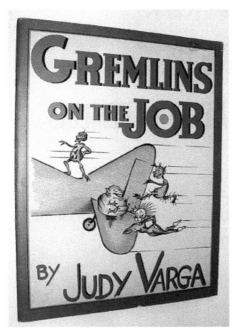

At first they sabotage the planes, but over time the humans make friends with them and they begin to repair the planes instead, so eventually they become an asset rather than a hindrance to aviation.

I think we have a gremlin on board just like those RAF planes did, and I call them the Health Gremlins. Over the years, mine has become a good friend because I feed him the right sort of food. He definitely has MoJo!

Our Health Gremlin feeds and thrives on emotions

Once it has devoured the emotion you are feeling, it morphs into that emotion, resulting in a state of health. This can be good health, bad health, or somewhere in-between. It all depends on what emotions you are feeding them.

It can be soothed, calmed and relaxed when we experience happiness, joy, contentment and pleasure.

It gets irritated, anxious, annoyed or angry when its human experiences worry, fear (real or imagined), guilt, low self-esteem, resentment and jealousy. No MoJo here!

Gremlinology is therefore the study of emotions and how they affect your Health Gremlin. Awareness of how you feed your Gremlin is crucial to your personal health and the well-being of both body and mind.

Recent neuroscience has shown us the clear connections between the mind and the body. When you have a thought about a situation or experience, that thought is filtered through your basic instincts (survival, sustenance, sex) and your personal life experiences, which teach you to gravitate towards pleasure and away from physical and emotional pain.

Resultant emotional chemicals are created by your hypothalamus gland and released into your bloodstream in milliseconds. This emotional 'food' is consumed by your Gremlin, resulting in its transformation so that it mirrors your feelings about the situation or experience.

Most people have heard of adrenaline (epinephrine in the USA) and know it primes you for the fight, flight or freeze reaction. This hormone is released when you think you are in trouble. It is initiated by a thought; this accounts for why some people react differently, (morphing different Gremlins) as they do not consider themselves to be challenged or in danger.

Individuals are also guided in life by their personal learned beliefs and values. It is vital that we all realise and appreciate the links between our personal thoughts, beliefs, values and words as all of these lead to our emotions and they are the meals our Gremlin feeds on.

The Way You Think Affects Your Gremlin

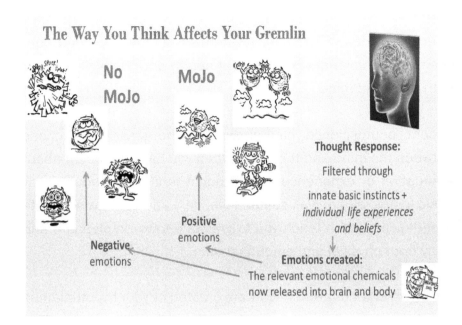

As you read through this book, you will develop more awareness of your own pressure points and begin to listen to them. Knowing yourself and your personal reactions may help you to start taking positive preventive measures.

There is a pressing health reason why we should all take this seriously. An angry, irritated Gremlin can settle into areas of your body that are particularly sensitive to lots of pressure:

- In the nervous system, the result could be headaches or migraines.
- In the muscular system, you could develop inflammation in your muscles and tendons, producing inflammatory pain and discomfort.

- In the skeletal system, it could affect joints, possibly resulting in arthritis or similar inflammatory conditions.
- In the liver, it could reduce the ability to handle toxins or affects one of the many other functions of this vital organ.

Health Gremlins reside in everyone. Your personal emotions determine whether the health outcome is pleasant, creating physical and mental well-being, or unpleasant, creating physical and mental ill health.

How often do you feed your Gremlin?
What emotions do you feed it?

It is impossible to avoid challenge or pressure in daily life; complete absence of pressures is achieved only when we die.

We humans need a reason to get up in the morning and regular challenges to keep us motivated. This results in an active interest in life, work and the environment around us. The person who has lost enthusiasm doesn't respond to a challenge and sees life as a depressing mountain of difficult routes and impossible climbs. Their Gremlin will mirror these emotions.

When you experience excessive pressures, it makes you feel out of balance and you begin to show symptoms of ill health (stress). This is a slow build up and can take weeks, months or years as your Gremlin feeds on a diet of resentment, unhappiness, anxiety, anger or worry (to mention a few).

There is a middle stage of adaptation where the body and your Gremlin begin to adapt to the physiological changes and pressures being experienced and attempts to restore 'normality'. The final stage of too much pressure (which is not always reached) is a serious illness: stroke, heart attack, mental breakdown or burnout.

On the other hand, the right level of pressure for you feels GREAT; you feel bright and happy and you are a lovely person to know! Your health is quite positive and you radiate your well-being to others (not all of whom appreciate it!). Your Gremlin has a diet of joy, hope, love, fun and generosity. You've got MoJo!

On my lecture tours, people ask me if they really get to choose between a happy or angry Gremlin. They say: "Surely our outlook and attitude is genetic?"

Take a look at how emotions are created (see the diagram on the previous page). Yes, there is a human genetic element. But the way you were brought up, the messages you learned and your perception from your life experiences, have had the most influence over your Gremlin's predominant state.

In my 18 years as a therapist, I have witnessed so many people learn how to change their thinking (and their Gremlin's diet) to create good health and well-being of body and mind; this has led me to my Healthy Gremlin Theory.

The home of the Health Gremlins is www.annmccracken.co.uk

"Every day we have plenty of
opportunities to get angry,
stressed or offended.
But what you're doing when you
indulge these negative emotions is
giving something outside yourself
power over your happiness.
You can choose to not let
little things upset you."

Joel Osteen

CHAPTER 3:

YOUR GREMLIN BECOMES WHAT IT EATS

We learned in the previous chapter that your Gremlin feeds on emotions.

Emotions create mental experiences that:

- Have a strongly motivating, subjective quality (like pleasure or pain);
- Are in response to some event or object that is either real or imagined; and,
- Motivate types of behaviour.

Some nations are historically more comfortable displaying emotion than others. The French, Spanish, Greeks and Turks as well as many Americans, are well known for showing affection, displeasure or enthusiasm through lots of excited, noisy laughter, joyous anticipation, tears and visible anger or disgust.

The British stiff upper lip says a lot about their stoicism and wish to "keep up appearances". This is still evident in the older generation in the UK, but the Millennials, or Y and Z demographics, appear to be less in favour of such stoicism and are undergoing a sea change in emotional freedom.

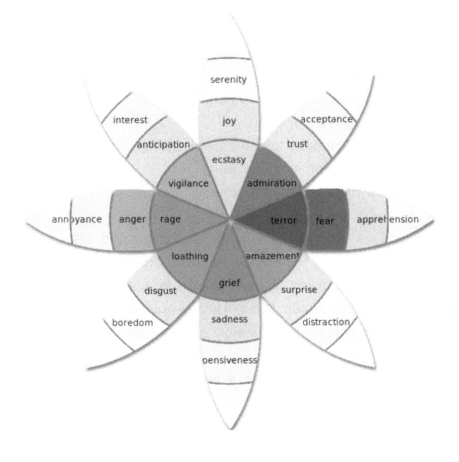

Will this mean their Gremlin will get access to different emotional chemicals resulting in a change in behaviour of the nation? An interesting concept!

Let's take a look at the most common emotions.

In 1980, Robert Plutchik constructed a flower diagram of emotions, visualising eight basic ones, plus eight derivative emotions, each comprising two basic ones. The eight basic emotions were:

- Joy
- Trust
- Fear
- Surprise
- Sadness
- Disgust
- Anger
- Anticipation

The resulting human feelings are displayed in the diagram's outer and inner limits.

Generations (approx.): Baby Boomers 1946-1964; Generation X 1965-1980; Millennials/Generation Y 1980-2002; Generation Z 2002-present

Extensive research has revealed many and varied lists of emotions, a much larger number than the above. For instance:

Absorbed	Confident	Exhilarated	Jealous	Resentful
Adoration	Confused	Fearful	Joyful	Restless
Afraid	Contempt	Fondness	Liking	Revulsion
Aggravated	Content	Frustrated	Lonely	Sad
Alarmed	Curious	Grief-stricken	Love	Safe
Alienated	Defeated	Grumpy	Lust	Satisfied
Amazed	Delighted	Guilty	Melancholy	Scared
Ambivalent	Depressed	Happy	Neglected	Scornful
Amused	Disappointed	Hateful	Nervous	Self-conscious
Angry	Disgraced	Helpless	Numb	Serenity
Anguished	Disgusted	Hesitant	Occupied	Shamed
Annoyed	Disillusioned	Hopeful	Optimistic	Shocked
Anticipating	Disliked	Hopeless	Outraged	Sorrow
Anxious	Dismayed	Horrified	Overwhelmed	Spiteful
Aroused	Disorientated	Hostile	Panicked	Stunned
Attracted	Distressed	Humiliated	Pity	Suspicious
Awkward	Disturbed	Hurt	Pleased	Sympathy
Bitter	Dread	Indifferent	Powerless	Tender
Bored	Eager	Infatuated	Proud	Tenderness
Brave	Elated	Inferior	Rage	Trust
Calm	Embarrassed	Insecure	Receptive	Trusting
Caring	Enthusiastic	Insulted	Regretful	Uncertain
Cautious	Envious	Interested	Rejected	Uncomfortable
Cheerful	Exasperated	Intrigued	Rejection	Vengeful
Comfortable	Excited	Irritated	Relaxed	Weary
Concern	Exhausted	Isolated	Relieved	Worried

Suffice to say that these emotions are an amazing diet for your Gremlin!

Whatever the emotion, when you experience it, based on your values and beliefs, your resultant personality, and the amount of pressure you believe you are experiencing in your current life, your Gremlin will eat the emotion and find the best place in your body where it can enjoy its meal.

If the emotion is pleasurable, joyous and comforting, this will feel nourishing and supporting and your Gremlin will be...

Where do you feel joy, elation, anticipation or optimism?

Where do you feel pain or discomfort when you are experiencing a lot of pressure

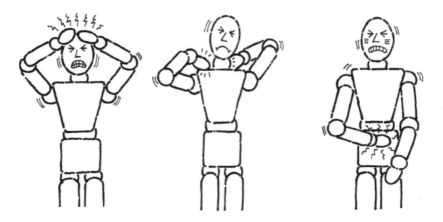

The idea that the way you think creates emotional chemicals which your Gremlin feeds on resulting in your health, is a novel and even challenging idea for some.

Western medicine has been based on cause and effect for hundreds of years, and as a microbiologist I have identified many organisms which cause disease. However, as I began to work with clients as a therapist, I became more and more aware of the power of the mind in human ill health – both physical and mental. There appears to be a different energy in people with a positive approach to life compared with those who expect the worst.

This has been confirmed in research by Barbara Fredrickson, who described in her book *Positivity*, how positive emotions increased an individual's personal resources. People who choose to change their outlook from negative to positive feed their Gremlin on a different set of emotions, for instance: love, joy, gratitude, serenity, interest, hope, pride, amusement, inspiration and awe, to mention just a few!

There are four major chemicals in the brain that influence our positivity/happiness:

- Dopamine is involved in the anticipation of the feeling of happiness
- Oxytocin is triggered through social bonding, eye contact and a cuddle
- Serotonin controls your mood – if you've got it, you feel great
- Endorphins soothe pain and discomfort, both physical and mental, resulting in you feeling more positive

Scientists have shown that activities like meditation, mindfulness, yoga, and Tai Chi create changes in emotional chemicals which can improve the immune system resulting in fewer colds, flus and infections. Your body is more energised, positive and resilient, and your Gremlin will be happy and healthy!

Such thinking is behind the current wave of Mindfulness training. Jon Kabat-Zinn brought Mindfulness into the mainstream of medicine and society. He is Professor of Medicine Emeritus and creator of the Stress Reduction Clinic and the Center for Mindfulness in Medicine, Health Care, and Society at the University of Massachusetts Medical School.

He defines mindfulness as:

"The awareness that emerges through paying attention on purpose, in the present moment, and non-judgementally to the unfolding of experience moment by moment."

Many parts of societies in the twenty-first century are frantic, hectic, fearful and anxious. They are time-poor and money-rich. This can affect both salaried workers undertaking long hours and hourly low-wage workers who work long hours to earn more money.

Eating and drinking out has flourished as evidenced by the increase in gastro pubs, restaurant chains and expensive restaurants. Many people seem to be chasing their tail to just keep their head above water and opportunities to 'just smell the flowers' are few and far between.

The emotions created from frantic, fearful and anxious lives are:

- Apprehension
- Guilt
- Regret
- Obsession
- Jealousy
- Envy
- Insecurity
- Exhilaration
- Arousal
- Depression

And no doubt many others! Each person will of course favour different reactions depending on their individual beliefs and the stories they habitually tell themselves.

Today, many have very limited time to 'stand and stare' as W H Davies so succinctly put it:

"What is this life if, full of care,
We have no time to stand and stare.
No time to stand beneath the boughs
And stare as long as sheep or cows."

"Calm mind brings inner strength and self-confidence,
so that's very important for good health."
Dalai Lama

But it is not just all about positive emotions; the way you express negative feelings can also be good for your health. Expressing how you feel and actively seeking to resolve the issue/s causing the feelings can result in positive change, a more stable emotional environment, and a composed Gremlin.

Sometimes when anger is repressed it becomes chronic and can result in cruelty or violence, leaving a trail of resentment, frustration, and guilt. Evidence is mounting that such behaviour may suppress the immune system which could allow the development of infections and even cancer cells.

It's not the emotion that's bad – it is how it is fed to your Gremlin.

"Learn to enjoy every
minute of your life.
Be happy now.
Don't wait for something
outside of yourself to make
you happy in the future.
Think how really precious
is the time you have to spend,
whether it's at work
or with your family.
Every minute should be
enjoyed and savored."

Earl Nightingale

CHAPTER 4:

YOU ARE WHAT YOU THINK AND SAY

Many of us have heard the phrase 'you are what you eat'. Foods contain combinations of nutrients, water and fibre. No single food can supply all nutrients in the amounts you need. A variety of foods are required and some have to be consumed in small amounts as they are relatively unhealthy and result in fat storage.

Your thoughts can be 'healthy' or 'unhealthy' in the same way...so you are the emotions your Gremlin eats. What do I mean by that?

Negativity

Negative and disempowering thoughts, e.g. I can't... this won't work... I couldn't... create emotional chemicals which make your Gremlin sad, anxious or unwell resulting in ill health in your body and mind.

Negativity is an underrated behaviour as it has lasting effects on individuals. It holds us back from being the best we can be as we will refrain from pushing ourselves out of our negative comfort zone with erroneous belief statements. And we'll repeat these limiting beliefs time and time again.

Positivity

A positive thought is powerful, motivating and empowering, e.g. I can... I will... this could work when I... These thoughts will create emotional chemicals which make your Gremlin happy and cheerful, and you'll feel empowered, resulting in health and well-being with resilience in both body and mind.

"Emotion (e-motion) is energy in motion."

This quote from Peter McWilliams and Robert Kiyosaki supports the physicist's view that everything is energy. Your thought is the initiator and the emotion created amplifies it; your actions in word or deed increase the momentum.

In the body, the energy can be positive or negative. You know how serious it is if you fuel your petrol vehicle with diesel instead? It is just as important to fuel your Gremlin with the best possible energy to keep yourself healthy and well. The best fuel/energy is POSITIVE! You feel your confidence rise. You laugh and smile more, which creates endorphins that soothe your Gremlin and keep your body optimised and harmonised.

Culture, myths and folklore have a strong influence on people, and sayings heard regularly in your childhood home become powerful beliefs even if your personal experience has proved otherwise. Statements learned when you are young are repeated in your head and out loud into adulthood. They become your emotional reality, even a mantra... They inform your thinking and this triggers emotions which feed your Gremlin and result in thoughts and consequent behaviours.

In the Western world, the body is often thought of as an intricate machine which must be kept tuned-up. Illness is viewed as a breakdown of the machine. We may not be sleek RAF planes like in Roald Dahl's children's book, but it seems that Gremlins aren't fussy and some of them have hitched a ride in our biological machines.

But this mechanistic view of health is not really fit for purpose. For example, for many centuries, awareness of emotions has not been thought relevant to good health – the power of the mind has not been harnessed to make and keep us well.

This contrasts with Eastern philosophies where health is perceived as a harmonious equilibrium that exists between the interplay of yin and yang. This Taoist concept sees yin and yang as two halves that together create wholeness. It is a dynamic equilibrium too, as yin and yang are continually waxing and waning, like the moon or the seasons of the year. It is depicted by this symbol named Taijitu, and exemplifies the holistic concept of oneness and equilibrium.

Just as the wheel of the year and the Tajitu keep turning, so your Gremlin continually morphs from one form into another depending on your emotions.

"Broadly speaking, Western society strives to find and prove the truth, while Eastern society accepts the truth as given and is more interested in finding the balance."

Vadim Kotelnikov and Anastasia Bibikova

You need a friend to help for this activity

1. **Stand with your feet slightly apart and raise your right or left arm until it is at right angles to your body.**
2. **Think about a great experience you had and really get re-involved in the joy, happiness, fun.**
3. **Ask your friend to push down on your arm while you resist.**
4. **Note the effect.**
5. **Now think of an unpleasant experience you had and feel it, see it, remember how it sounded.**
6. **Ask your friend to repeat the arm pressure while you try to resist.**
7. **Note the change.**

The difference is usually dramatic.
When thinking positively, it is easy to resist.
When thinking negatively, it is hard to resist the same pressure and your arm is easily pushed down.

Demonstrating positive and negative states

The previous exercise clearly demonstrates how your body becomes de-energised when you feel negative and low.

Kinesiologists test muscles in this way. Kinesiology is a relatively recent therapeutic practice that uses muscle testing to determine what techniques will help bring your body back into balance. It is a holistic approach, detecting the whole body's response.

Advice on how to keep your gremlin happy

1. Check in with your attitude regularly – is it positive or negative?
2. If you are in a negative state, encourage yourself to think about a good time or a positive experience.
3. When you are smiling again, you know you are back in a positive state and are more likely to make good decisions or have good judgement.

You do not need to be tested by a kinesiologist to be aware of your whole body feelings. You know what it feels like to be in a positive or a negative state. The visualisation of a positive state in the exercise demonstrates how much we are able to influence our body states. Sport psychologists at the top levels have encouraged their athletes to access a positive, winning state. Now you can too!

Beliefs

Our beliefs provide a moral framework, set preferences and give us a steer on our relationships.

Examples of beliefs are:

- Prejudice
- Biase
- Intolerance
- Honesty
- Reliable
- Open
- Accountable
- Progressive

Every moment of every day, our brain is processing information and this is influenced by our belief systems. Our beliefs originate from all our life experiences and what we were told as children by our family, friends and wider society. Matthew Lieberman, a psychologist at the University of California, showed in 2005 how beliefs help people's brains categorise others and view objects as good or bad, largely unconsciously. He demonstrated that beliefs (in this case, prejudice or fear) are most likely to be learned from the prevailing culture.

Words and thoughts are the seeds of action and actions become habits. Words announce to the world how you feel and what you think about important values; these determine what emotions your Gremlin will eat and how it/you will behave.

Case Study: the Gremlin soother

One of my clients was an elderly lady who was going into hospital for a significant operation. It was the first one she had ever needed to have and she was absolutely petrified; every time she presented for the op, her blood pressure was sky-high and she displayed such strong signs of anxiety that her doctors had to send her home.

By chance, we met in our village where she told me of her conundrum. I suggested I work with her to devise a method to manage her blood pressure so that the operation could go ahead. It was simple – I taught her diaphragmatic breathing and made her a CD full of positive statements and outcomes to listen to before, during and after the operation.

It worked! Deep breathing done correctly slows down the respiratory and circulatory systems and allows the body and mind to calm down and recuperate. Her Gremlin then fed on the positive words on the CD and so created emotions of calm and peace.

It was not just the CD that worked; it was also her open-minded attitude.

At the grand old age of 81, she was willing to try something new. Her positive belief that she could take control of her fear was what really did the trick! Her changed way of thinking affected her life and her Gremlin. It had morphed into a relaxed and comfortable state, even when she was in the operating theatre.

This happened 15 years ago and diaphragmatic breathing and mindfulness is now well established as a Gremlin soother.

"I try to make my mood uplifting and peaceful, then watch the world around me reflect that mood."

Yaya DaCosta

CHAPTER 5:

HOW FOOD AFFECTS YOUR MOOD

Your Gremlin feeds on emotions and feelings (see Chapter 1). Emotions power our reactions, which can be indifferent or intense, strong or weak. When we perceive ourselves to be experiencing a lot of pressure, the chemicals associated with stress increase and symptoms follow.

Sometimes the reaction or coping strategy to lots of pressure is to reach for food... It is a well-known fact that carbohydrates (or carbs as they are affectionately known) produce a feel-good factor which has been related to the brain chemical serotonin.

This is what happens:

- Carbs cause the body to release more insulin.
- One of insulin's properties is to promote removal of some amino acids but to leave tryptophan in the blood.
- Serotonin is made from the amino acid tryptophan.

As well as lots of other biological functions, serotonin is believed to promote mood balance between happiness and depression hence the feel-good factor.

Consequently, we have learned to overeat carbohydrates to make ourselves feel better, particularly snack foods like potato chips or pastries, which are rich in carbohydrates and fats.

This Gremlin doesn't care how serotonin is made, it just loves to get lots of it and be happy!

Serotonin isn't found in foods but tryptophan is, so we need to eat to get the basic chemicals to make it. Food like eggs, nuts, seeds, tofu, salmon, turkey, watercress, spinach and spirulina are rich in tryptophan. Perhaps it's worth taking this route to make serotonin rather than the well-worn carb route.

Omega-3 fatty acids can also influence mood, behaviour and personality. They are found in flax seeds, walnuts, sardines, salmon, grass-fed beef, soybeans, prawns, Brussels sprouts and cauliflower.

Low blood levels of polyunsaturated omega-3 fatty acids are associated with depression, bipolar disorder, schizophrenia, and attention deficit disorder.

Studies have found that diets low in carbohydrates increased feelings of anger, depression and tension, and diets high in carbohydrates have a generally uplifting effect on mood so it is not surprising that we reach for the carbs when we spend all day confronting challenging mental tasks. In this situation, the brain's nutritional demands are greater, but physical activity is often lower.

We produce lots of oxidants in the brain when we are working hard and foods that are high in antioxidants – berries, beans, apples, tea – act to neutralise these potentially damaging chemicals. These could be the healthy answer to influencing your mood.

Coffee, tea and energy drinks

All these drinks contain varying levels of caffeine and the scientific literature seems to agree that caffeine increases serotonin levels in the brain, but it doesn't increase serotonin production. At any given time, most of the brain's serotonin is stored in nerve cells, waiting to be released and caffeine is one of the triggers for its release. Caffeine's main effect is to counteract the sedating effect of other brain chemicals and this important balance can be disturbed by excess caffeine. The body is a finely tuned instrument and anything in excess will significantly change this balance.

Given that you now know that caffeine affects serotonin levels in the brain, you should make sure of a few things if you intend to continue to take caffeine on a regular basis (whether you drink energy drinks, black coffee, or green tea).

Caffeine acts like a drug. While it may give you more energy and make you feel more alert, there are naturally downsides to regular use of this stimulant.

Too much caffeine can increase your blood pressure and blood sugar as well as inducing insomnia. However, other studies have suggested that it improves memory and concentration as well as lowering the risk of Alzheimer's and liver cancer.

Another interesting fact is many people consume chocolate when they are in negative moods such as boredom, anger, depression and tiredness, but it is also consumed at times of joy and happiness. Dark chocolate, containing 85% cocoa, may increase serotonin levels not only due to the serotonin and L-tryptophan it contains, but also because it contains carbohydrates in the form of sugar, which can signal the body to produce more serotonin.

Your Gremlin enjoys being happy and cheerful or angry and irrational and it's your choice what you feed it for your best physical and psychological health.

How does food affect your Gremlin?

Only you know how you react to food. If it is a pleasurable feeling, your Gremlin will be happy and satiated; if it is accompanied by angst and fear, these are the emotions your Gremlin will consume.

This concept is echoed by the work of Marc David at the Institute for the Psychology of Eating, Colorado:

"The mind has a profound influence on the body when it comes to how we metabolize a meal."

The environment in which you eat is also important. Grabbing a sandwich at your desk means there are many other demands for your attention and the food you eat is relegated to secondary or even a mindless position. This may create a neutral or negative state in your brain and your chemical reactions will be downgraded accordingly. Your Gremlin may be starved of emotion.

So now you know that it is not just what you eat but how and why you eat it!

This leads me to food addiction. Currently, about 12 million people in the UK suffer from compulsive overeating to some extent. Food can feel like an addiction – a desire to eat something that is forbidden.

Binge and compulsive overeaters often describe themselves as lacking in willpower to resist tempting adverts, coffee shop cakes, biscuits and coffee add-ons like cream and syrups, and 'mega' deals, which usually double the size of a meal. Fast food is laced with sugar, and consumers will usually say that they are eating for comfort rather than for genuine physical need.

This may produce a happy Gremlin for a short while but then the self-loathing or disgust kicks in and that creates a very different Gremlin...

Other important food/health 'habits'

1.   Drink water. Research* suggests the brain and heart are composed of 73% water, the lungs are approximately 83% water, the skin contains 64% water, and the muscles and kidneys are 79% water.

When the body is active and awake for 10 to 12 hours a day, removing metabolic waste from the brain requires optimal hydration.

Regular intake of pure water is essential to dilute dehydrators like processed sugary foods, high doses of caffeine, and sweet carbonated drinks.

Your Gremlin likes to float around your body and needs water to find the emotions it loves to consume – whatever they are!

2.   Chew your food well. Plants have cellulose cell walls and this requires lots of chewing to access the goodness inside the cells. Cellulose is a good source of fibre which keeps your digestive system active, cleansed and healthy. Chewing releases the nutrients inside the cells and the nutrients become available more quickly and efficiently to provide you with sustenance.

Poorly chewed food takes longer to be digested, using energy which could be put to better use in the body.

Chewing is a contemplative activity as it (should) stop us talking; leaving time to focus on and savour the food we are eating.

You don't need to sit like the Yoga Gremlin...but taking your time and noticing what you are eating is really good for you!

3.   Develop/keep a positive attitude in your daily life and your interactions with others. Speak openly about your emotions and have them validated. Such positivity creates great emotional 'food' for your Gremlin and helps it feel energised.

However, it is not always about binges and compulsive eating – some people find it difficult to eat enough food to sustain them...

*Ottley, C. 2000. Food and mood. Nursing Standard, 15(2): 46-52.

Case Study: Erin's eating problems

Erin was a successful young woman in the fast, competitive arena of PR, who presented at my clinic with eating problems. She was unable to eat very much and did not like to eat in public. This caused problems in the personal, social and work areas of her life. We explored her relationship with food, how this affected her thinking and the emotions that were created around this vital, life-sustaining component. Over a period of months, she practiced self-awareness, becoming aware of her thinking about food, her thoughts when she was around food, and the messages she had heard about food when she was growing up. She decided to work with her Gremlin to change her reactions.

Very quickly, she learned to be aware of the emotions she was feeding her Gremlin and through mindfulness exercises, she began to practice using different emotional reactions to food. This gave her the courage to practice eating with friends and family. She continued working hard on changing her thoughts and noticing changed emotions until one day it became natural to eat enough to sustain her with occasional treats.

Her relationship improved; her strength of mind also, with a positive effect on her work and home life. She set up in private practice and turned her hobby into a successful business.

Your MoJo is nourished by your relaxed control around food showing you enjoy eating but know when to eat and when to stop.

CHAPTER 6:
HEALTH GREMLINS AND STRESS

Stress is a word that is ill-defined. As I circuit the UK providing training for organisations, I have discovered there are many different ideas of what 'stress' is.

People talk about 'good' stress and 'bad' stress, stressful experiences and 'stressy' behaviours.

Stress is certainly related to the emotions that we considered in Chapter 3. Let's make it crystal clear... stress is an adverse health reaction when you perceive you have too much pressure. A bit of pressure is good for you – it keeps you on your toes and your Gremlin loves it because it creates positive emotions!

Too much pressure makes you unwell or ill (stress) and your Gremlin will reflect your feelings of ill health.

You may have noticed that people react differently in the same situation. Each of us reacts differently because we all have variations in our physiology (internal body workings), as well as differences in our beliefs, thinking patterns and life experiences. Remember: your Gremlin will eat every emotion you give to it.

It is my experience that most people have a diagnostic system – a part of your body that always goes wrong when you are under lots of pressure. It's an indication that one of your systems is less effective than the others and this is where health problems appear first.

For example, you:

- Are asthmatic (respiratory and immune system);
- Experience skin problems like eczema, psoriasis or dermatitis (skin and Immune system);
- Get muscle tension or back problems (skeletal system);
- Have high blood pressure (cardiac system);
- Have angina or other heart conditions (cardiac system);
- Experience digestive upsets such as Irritable Bowel Syndrome or Colitis (digestive system);
- Are very nervous, worry lots or get anxious and often have headaches/migraines (nervous system).

One or more of these conditions will often get worse when you are seriously challenged or concerned by personal issues, work or a family problem.

This is your Gremlin at work, eating your emotional chemicals and finding your weak spot.

Now think very carefully...when you are upset by something or someone, how does it make you feel? What part of your body tells you it is distressed?

This helps you see where your Gremlin resides:

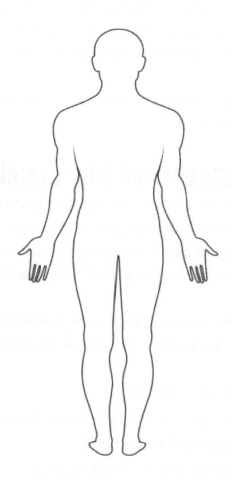

Draw a Gremlin in the area/s where stress affects YOU.

Stress is very personal; where it affects us varies from person to person. In the same way, how we react to pressure depends on our personal biological system.

DNA profiling has shown that unless you are an identical twin, no one else has the same profile. Siblings are similar but differences are recognisable.

Our DNA dictates how our systems function and there are many minor variations which is one of the reasons we may react differently to drugs, treatments and a lot of pressure.

By identifying how your body reacts to pressure, you will begin to become more self-aware.

Messages from your Gremlin

Most of us know when we are being challenged and how we react, but we are sometimes much too good at ignoring it. Some people just accept they suffer from headaches, stomach upsets or panic attacks without questioning what their body is telling them.

Such symptoms are a message from your Health Gremlin that you need to review your situation.

Good questions to ask would be:
- When do I get these headaches/stomach aches/back aches/sadness/fear/anxiety?
- What/who is currently upsetting me?
- What can I do about it?

Our Western medicine tends to treat symptoms rather than causes so treatments are reactive and usually medicine based. Taking stock of all the situations/people/thinking styles around the time of these symptoms and our reaction to all of these influences can be extremely illuminating.

Negative internal states often occur just before the manifestation of ill health and the link with your Gremlin becomes obvious. The derangement of the body's immune system, a reduction in hydration due to distress or overthinking, will allow systems to malfunction and/or viruses, bacteria and fungi to thrive.

Case Study: Liam's ME

Liam was a budding young athlete until he was diagnosed with ME (Myalgic Encephalomyelitis). This condition affected his muscles and depleted his energy big time! He was devastated and lost all his self-belief, confidence and his MoJo.

He didn't look ill, he was just tired and desperately missing the buzz he got from training and winning races.

ME may occur after a viral infection and his mum remembered he'd had 'some sort of virus' just over a year before which had hampered his training programme at the time.

With his doctor's agreement, we began a programme of a healthy Mediterranean style diet, self-awareness, positive self-belief and self-confidence, using anchoring techniques to ground him back in his earlier successes while building on his current academic successes at school.

He slowly became fitter and his blood markers for ME reduced. He returned to training in athletics which was his passion but now he continually monitored his physical well-being when he trained because he knew how vital this information was to his long-term health.

CHAPTER 7:

SOOTHING YOUR GREMLIN

Life today is highly charged for many people:

- High-speed travel on planes, trains, bikes, cars
- Running or cycling to work
- Constant accessibility on mobiles, tablets, e-mail, video calls, and even watches!
- Must-have clothes, phones, homes, holidays, cars, accessories

Fast response times are expected both at work and on a personal level. It has become the norm to dodge people walking along the street who are engaged on their mobile in some sort of communication or game. Constant stimulation seems to be the order of the moment.

On top of that, there is a 24-hour blitz of world news, bringing us scary information about bombings, blasts, deaths, murder and maiming as well as national disasters, economic challenges and fleeing refugees.

The initial result of all these events on our body is 'fight, flight or freeze', with powerful chemicals rampaging through our systems to make us alert and ready to respond to the challenge...but the challenge is not physical... It is psychological and this constant overstimulation will overload your Gremlin.

Psychological overload results in physical and mental exhaustion (stress) and the outcomes are different for each individual as we all have a different physiology.

The result is often anxiety and dysfunctional responses such as overeating and drinking, poor quality of sleep, poor concentration and memory loss, tears, anger, and withdrawn behaviour, panic attacks, headaches, high blood pressure and loss of libido. Some people develop workaholic behaviour while others take legal and/or illegal drugs. These people may still be at work but their productivity will be severely reduced; this is called presenteeism which is 'the practice of coming to work despite illness, injury, anxiety, etc, often resulting in reduced productivity' (from Dictionary.com). Absences also increase, resulting in sanctions at work which pile on more personal pressure...and your Gremlin is deeply unhappy and absolutely worn out!

How can we soothe our Gremlin and restore it to a contented yet alert state?

It is a fact that if you keep doing what changed your good health to ill health, nothing will change...so you will have to change what you are doing!

This is not easy, neither is it impossible. It requires awareness and commitment that you need to do things differently.

- You can't just stop e-mailing
- You can't just stop taking/making calls
- You just can't stop seeing news bulletins/ newspaper headlines
- You just can't stop travelling long journeys in trains, planes and cars
- You just can't stop caring for people who depend on you

What you can do is:

- Clarify your priorities
- Set other people's expectations
- Limit your exposure to news if it upsets you – there is always an OFF button on communication appliances
- Use your time to create a tiny space for peace and tranquillity
- Ask others, or pay for support for your family and people who depend on you – you don't need to do everything yourself.

A great way to nurture your Gremlin is to take 20 seconds regularly (at least once an hour) to breathe deeply from your diaphragm.

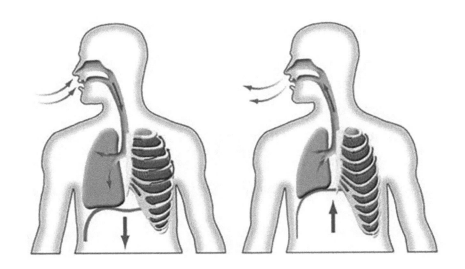

- **Place your hand on your midriff, just below your chest**
- **Take a deep breath in through your nose and be aware that your hand is being pushed outwards by your diaphragm**
- **This is often described as 'breathing into your stomach or abdomen'**
- **Blow out through your mouth**
- **Allow the exhale to continue for as long as possible**
- **Check that your shoulders are not raised and tense. They need to be relaxed and the breath going into the abdominal area**
- **REPEAT at least five times**

This can be done when standing, sitting, walking, lying down, with eyes open or closed. In other words, you can do this anywhere, anytime, anyplace.

By focusing on the act of breathing for a short time – feeling the air move in and out, hearing the sound of your exhale and inhale – this allows you to clear your mind, aerate your body systems (and your Gremlin), resulting in increased energy for you and your Gremlin. You become more perceptive and aware after this simple exercise.

This is the basis of Mindfulness and, once you have focused your breathing on your Gremlin, you are also strengthening your muscles and your mind.

If you choose to, you can continue this practice further by noticing what and who is around you with relaxed curiosity. You can notice sounds, smells, movement, texture, your own feelings and thoughts without making any judgement.

You can think of something that happens every day more than once; something you take for granted, like opening a door, or starting up your computer/laptop. The moment you touch the doorknob/laptop or object, stop for a moment and be mindful of where you are, how you feel in that moment and what the next step is. As you perform the task, take a moment to appreciate the simple process and the amazing brain that facilitates your action and understanding.

This will help you to cultivate mental spaciousness for your Gremlin and achieve a positive mind-body balance.

It is so easy to incorporate this approach into your daily life and if you choose to do this, the effect will be to soothe your Gremlin, as well as calming your body and mind and boosting your MoJo.

Case study: Jill's frazzled Gremlin

'Jill' presented with worry and anxiety. She was not sleeping well, and she was losing weight and feeling sick. While chatting, I discovered she was very worried about 'the world'. She felt that the news bulletins were full of disasters, economic worries, 'bad people' and climate concerns. She and her Gremlin were 'frazzled' (a technical term!) and serious soothing was required.

We discussed switching off the TV or radio but her husband would then miss out, so she came up with the idea of leaving the room, closing the door and going to a different part of their home and listening to her favourite music or an audio book... She thought 'everyone' would think she was weird and when I asked her who else lived in the house, it transpired that the two of them lived on their own.

She then decided she did not need to tell 'everyone', and a few weeks later she looked and felt so much better on her new regime.

Soothing your Gremlin is good for your mental and physical health!

CHAPTER 8:

LIVING WITH A POSITIVE GREMLIN

Do you like to feel free, happy, joyous, contented, satiated, abundant, respectful and cheerful? These and your own personal take on happiness, is how it feels to live with a positive Gremlin.

Recent research on happiness has clarified that people who tend to leave towards a positive, optimistic and realistic outlook are healthier and more satisfied with their life.

Using the Gremlin analogy, it is feeding on emotional chemicals which energise and nourish it.

A few years ago, a neuroscience researcher, Dr Candace Pert, discovered what she called the 'molecules of emotion'. She was able to describe them chemically as well as identify which organ they targeted! Here, at last, was the connection between the brain/mind and the body!

Imagine a piece of Velcro with one side consisting of tiny hooks and the other side with acceptors for the hooks; Dr Pert found that a few compounds associated with the emotion had specific hooks for acceptors on various human organs.

This means that the emotional chemical associated with elation has a specific place or places in the body where it lodges.

Where do you feel elation? Some people tell me they feel it in their facial muscles which involuntarily creates a smile, not only around the mouth but in the eyes; other muscles in the body also react creating a positive stance and general brightness along with a feeling of joy. Just imagine your Gremlins morphing into a happy state and all working together to create this feeling of elation!

To keep a Gremlin positive and achieve MoJo, you need to learn that being positive is a choice. In any situation, there is an opportunity to think negatively or positively. It is up to each of us to determine how to make the best of the situation by taking personal responsibility for how we feel and accepting how we feel. By taking control of our attitude, we enable our Gremlin to help us find the positive in every situation.

No matter how bad things are, there is always something to learn from every experience, and taking this attitude will begin to feed your Gremlin positive feelings and make you more able to cope.

This enabling state creates more confidence as well as a mindset of abundance, enthusiasm, and the ability to create solutions – all of which means your Gremlin will morph into even more positive, happy and engaging Gremlins – what's not to want about that!

The concept of mindfulness – or living in the moment – allows us to focus on what is happening NOW. It allows us to pay attention to who we are with, or what we are doing, or how we are feeling thus giving our Gremlin a clear steer on how we want to feel. By taking every waking hour as it comes, doing what you are supposed to do, and completing what you have tasked yourself with, you have done your best and this will feed your Gremlin with happy and contented emotions.

Even when life is hurtful, you can take a tiny time out to focus on the wonders in your life – your sleeping child, your smooth silky cat or your loving, grateful dog, even the beautiful wavy or straight hair of the person sitting in front of you. There is so much beauty and simple pleasure to be found when we live in the moment and feed these feelings to our Gremlin.

Interestingly, some people sabotage their positive Gremlin by introducing doubt. They feel they are not worthy of such great feelings or that by allowing themselves to enjoy an experience, somehow that will lead to great disappointment. This suggests they allow their Gremlin to morph into the more negative aspects of their personality.

**"A pessimist sees the difficulty
in every opportunity;
an optimist sees
the opportunity
in every difficulty."**

Winston Churchill

Living with a negative Gremlin

Stress (physical and mental ill health) is associated with feelings like guilt, sadness, anger, fear, regret, shame and the 'victim' state. Everyone will have their own personal collection of emotional chemicals, based on negative beliefs and life experiences.

If you constantly feed it negative thoughts and feelings, your Gremlin will forget how to morph into its positive counterpart.

Constantly feeling under lots of pressure (real or imagined) creates the emotions and behaviours associated with negativity – hostility, uncommunicative, awkward, resentful, envious, indifferent, anxious and depressed.

Using the Gremlin analogy, it is feeding on emotional chemicals which are de-energising, creating unpleasant Gremlins in your body. This has the effect of making your body systems less effective, resulting in ill health of various types.

Experiencing failure provides an opportunity to wallow in self-pity and feed the emotions of disappointment and sadness to your Gremlin who will lap it up willingly.

However, failure can also be seen as a learning opportunity of what does not work and the chance to try something else; this provides hope and interest, fostering creative thinking, resulting in positive chemicals with a very different outcome for your Gremlin.

**"Only those who dare to fail greatly
can ever achieve greatly."**

Robert F. Kennedy

The habit of worrying and overanalysing is also a choice! Worrying about a situation or person has no effect whatsoever on the outcome and it feeds your Gremlin with fear, despair and angst, all of which are negative chemicals which create ill health.

Sometimes we hold on to our anger at someone, believing that somehow it will upset the person you are mad at and they will realise they have hurt you. Unfortunately, all that happens is that your Gremlin begins to burn up with the angry emotions and may even add some more hate and fear, animosity and loathing.

This is very destructive to your body and your Gremlin needs to be soothed with forgiving thoughts and actions. Allow the anger to reduce hour by hour so that you and your Gremlin become strong and healthy again.

Case Study: John's anxiety

'John' was a worrier. There was very little that he didn't worry about. He worried about the state of the traffic on his way to work, whether or not he would get a parking spot in the car park or have to park 'outside' where his car could be damaged. He worried about the moods of his colleagues and if they would be supportive. He had heard there was the possibility of a takeover of the business and the insecurity was worrying him, even though everyone else said their jobs were safe. In his open-plan office, there was a large monitor that constantly relayed world news and he worried about terrorism, wars, refugees, political decisions, local and international disasters, and the state of the currency.

He had quite a few health issues; he had Irritable Bowel Syndrome which was so painful that sometimes he had to take time off work. He occasionally had panic attacks, often found his concentration was poor, and found making simple decisions challenging. He had regular colds, succumbed to other infections and was putting on weight due to overeating.

When we put all these symptoms together, he was horrified and refused to accept that there was any connection. I explained how he was feeding his health Gremlin and slowly it all fell into place.

We made a plan to tackle his issues sequentially, and I am glad to say that six months later, he was much improved in physical and emotional health! Now he had a clear goal.

CHAPTER 9:
GREMLINS AND TECHNOLOGY

**"In today's rush, we all think too much —
seek too much — want too much —
and forget about the joy of just being."
Eckhart Tolle**

Gremlins have traditionally been associated with technical things going wrong, but as described here, your personal Gremlin is exactly what you feed it emotionally, thus introducing an aspect of personal responsibility.

However, in the twenty-first century, technology has stealthily taken over our lives. Interestingly it morphs so quickly into something new almost as fast as your Gremlin does.

We have developed a 'throw away or upgrade' society as the demographic generations designated as X, Y and Z regularly change or upgrade their technology and communication equipment. They rapidly absorb the changed technology, often at significant expense.

They are extremely savvy in the use of technological advances, leaping lithely from Facebook to Instagram to Hive to Spotify, new apps, drones, robotics and other applications of artificial intelligence.

There are three key aspects to these recent technological developments and their effect on people:

1. The pressure to keep up and sport the latest technology
2. The addictive usage of the equipment
3. The increased range of communication, facilitating our lives and homes in many useful ways

The right amount of pressure for an individual is good and healthy. However, what is 'right' for one person is not necessarily 'right' for someone else.

Demographic X born: 1965-1976; Demographic Y born: 1980-2000; Demographic Z born: 2000-present

The right amount of pressure stimulates, motivates and results in a good effort or performance without overstretching the individual's resources. The individual is happy and feels in control.

Excessive pressures, on the other hand, either from others or self-induced, have a very different effect, resulting in physical or psychological ill health and a sense of constantly chasing your tail.

In the light of this information, how do the three aspects above affect you and the society you live in?

1.   The pressure to keep up and sport the latest technology

Constantly trying to show off and be competent with the latest technology puts a lot of strain on an individual's resources, both monetarily and psychologically. It enhances the natural competitive behaviour we have as humans, sometimes to the level of totally focused intensity which supersedes the basic human needs. The individual becomes dehydrated, ignores food or only eats fast food, thus overdosing on sugar and reducing a lot of essential vitamins and minerals; their interpersonal skills are reduced to digital communication. And demonstrating those hard won technical skills could result in envy or dislike from their (digital) peers.

The result is their Gremlin is being fed emotions of arrogance, smugness and vanity, which are not really sought-after traits in society.

The body the Gremlin inhabits could be starved of some nutrients, thus making internal body communication sluggish and less effective

2.   Obsessive or addictive use of technology

The key psychological issue with much of this technological equipment is the addictive behaviour it seems to generate in some users. It is being recognised throughout the world. The addiction is seen across all demographics, as people walk along pavements, across streets, in shops etc. with heads bowed and thumbs active. Phones can be set to vibrate in pockets or bags and watches can tap your wrist to let you know that an e-mail or text has arrived. They can monitor your activity level and even tell you when to stand or breathe!

Addicted individuals experience a significant high (increased elation and deep involvement) when using computers, games, tablets and phones. It's similar to amphetamines and cocaine which stimulate the brain's reward system.

And they too feel withdrawal when cut off from their drug of choice.

It's not simply the amount of time spent with the digital device that defines the behaviour, but how excessive use adversely affects their Gremlin and thus their mental and physical health, daily life, relationships and academic or job performance.

This behaviour has been defined as iDisorder by Dr Larry Rosen, Professor Emeritus and Past Chair of the Psychology Department at California State University.

He indicates that neuroscientists have shown changes to the brain's ability to process information and reduced ability to relate to the world.

Symptoms can include:

- Compulsive checking of text messages
- Frequent changing of Facebook status and uploading of selfies
- A feeling of euphoria while on the Web
- Social withdrawal
- Loss of interest in activities that don't involve a computer, phone or gadget
- Feelings of restlessness when unable to go online
- Regular checking of availability of appropriate cables for phones, tablets, watches etc.
- Phantom vibrations in their pockets!

Dr Rosen suggests that these are indicative of serious psychological conditions e.g. narcissism, obsessive compulsive disorder, addiction, attention deficit disorder, social phobia, antisocial personality disorder, hypochondriasis, body dysmorphic disorder, schizo-disorders, and voyeurism.

However, he has a positive note to make on this concerning development, namely that the brain has neuroplasticity – the ability to change and accommodate some of these behaviours. This may mean that we can learn not to overuse the technology and use it in moderation. However, we need to want to moderate the behaviour for this to be effective!

3. The increased range of communication

There are obvious communication advantages to internet-based technology for all demographic groups; for instance, the ability to access any form of information, day or night, has revolutionised how people and businesses communicate. You can buy anything over the internet and pay for it easily, manage your bank account and move money with ease, access live news bulletins and trade stocks and shares, book a show, holiday or table at a restaurant from any place in the world. You can keep in touch with family and friends around the world using FaceTime and Skype. You can organise your home heating and check your security remotely, which can ease anxiety.

Once you have mastered these activities, your Gremlin will be fed with your reactive emotions of success on achieving a task. I find it extremely useful to use internet banking, which has revolutionised accounting, payments and the use of time. However, like all internet-based activities, it is open to attack. An aggressive virus can be devastating, distressing and disastrous for your personal communication or business.

I minimise this as much as possible, and give it positive rather than negative energy (and I keep my fingers crossed!).

When technology is challenging, it encourages the brain to work to its full potential, which is an interesting by-product for all generations. Innovative people have created opportunities to set up 'virtual' companies, work from home and cooperate with others. Companies that started like this are now household names like Google, Apple, Facebook, Microsoft and Amazon.

Another example of such innovation is the Kickstarter community, which uses the internet to help creative people of all ages get funding for their projects. On this platform, creative developers post projects seeking funding from the community, which then helps to create new jobs.

The innovative concept of storing information in a virtual 'cloud' is still challenging for many of the older generation (demographically called Baby Boomers) whose use of this technology is low. However, efforts are in hand to make this as 'safe' as possible.

Case Study: Hina's addiction

'Hina' loved her tablet and smartphone and the freedom they gave her to organise her social life and keep in touch with family and friends through Facebook and FaceTime. She had the latest version of her phone and a lovely case to protect it from damage. At night, in bed, she would watch music videos, episodes of her favourite comedy shows, catch up on the soaps and the occasional film.

It took up a lot of her time and she became isolated from her immediate family, only texting friends but seldom meeting up. She wasn't sleeping very well and had recently noticed she had shoulder and neck pain, which she put down to sitting in a draught.

One day whilst on her way to the supermarket, she was checking her texts when she walked into the side of a moving car she hadn't noticed. It frightened the driver and gave her pains in her chest and arm. She dropped her phone and was more concerned about whether it was damaged than her own injuries. A paramedic diagnosed a broken forearm and severe shock and she was taken to hospital.

We discussed many pointers that led her to appreciate the effects of her addictive behaviour on her physical and psychological health, as well as her sleep deprivation and relationships. She resolved to reduce the omnipresent distraction of her technology and revisit hobbies she had given up. She vowed to feed her Gremlin a more varied diet so that she could reinvigorate her MoJo.

CHAPTER 10:

LIFE EXPERIENCES

**"Life is a succession of lessons which
must be lived to be understood."
Ralph Waldo Emerson**

In my private practice and as a trainer, I spend a significant amount of time listening to people's perception of their life experiences.

There are many life experiences:

- Belonging (relationships)
- Doing (meaningful engagement in activities)
- Childhood
- School/college/university
- Employment
- Falling in/out of love
- Parenthood
- Travel/living in another country
- Becoming competent in music, sport, language,
- Bereavement

Life experiences are learnings that can only be described, felt, or heard when you experience a situation for yourself. Your life experiences are YOUR reality.

When you were growing up, your parents or carers influence your thinking and expectations of how the 'world' is. They instil a beliefs and value systems.

These life beliefs and values can be challenged as soon as you enter the school system and meet others with differing life experiences. These challenges continue through the teenage years into adulthood when you begin to make up your mind as to which beliefs and values work for you.

This process only happens in an individual who has been given permission to explore life and what it means to them. Some societies do not give this permission, and bring up their offspring in a closed or semi-closed society with strict instructions on how to uphold the family/group/religion's rules and beliefs.

Your personal life experiences along with your innate basic instincts (which keep you safe) will therefore inform the emotions you feel and then feed your Gremlin.

Let me remind you of this diagram from earlier in the book...

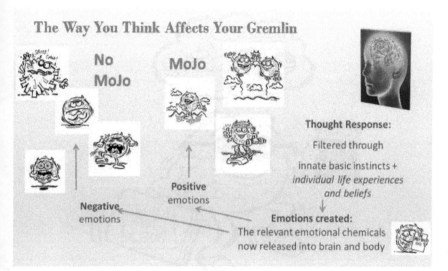

The Way You Think Affects Your Gremlin

No MoJo

MoJo

Negative emotions

Positive emotions

Thought Response:

Filtered through

innate basic instincts + *individual life experiences and beliefs*

↓

Emotions created:
The relevant emotional chemicals now released into brain and body

Your Gremlin will morph from one form to another depending on the emotions you feed it. This can feel quite confusing. You can have a variety of feelings coursing through your brain and body when a situation is emotionally challenging.

Let's take a look at one of these life experiences to see how it can affect emotions and our personal awareness.

How do you feel about travelling?

The UK is not a large country yet I still find people are surprised that I happily travel anywhere in Scotland, England, Wales and Northern Ireland on my own, if necessary on public transport or in my car. This suggests to me that not everyone is comfortable with travel, locally or further afield. It is therefore worth visiting this topic to appreciate how it affects your Gremlin.

Any distance of travel requires planning

Planning will give your Gremlin security. Security is a comfortable emotion, but can easily be dislodged by nervousness and insecurity if the plan goes wrong.

When plans go wrong we have two options:

- Panic, throw a tantrum, become agitated and anxious, or
- Make a new plan

The option you take will be based on the beliefs and values instilled when you were young.

However, they may also be affected if you are travelling with someone else or a group.

The panic option is an emotional one, possibly based on lack of previous experience, insecurity or even arrogance as expectations have not been met. These are definitely emotions your Gremlin can use to morph into a different, rather unhelpful personality. Making a new plan is an effective coping strategy, allowing your Gremlin to feed on active, positive energy, creating new solutions from flexible and creative thinking, resulting in confidence and self-awareness which are good behaviours to rely on when travelling.

Once you have done your planning, there is still a lot of opportunity to immerse yourself in angst and anxiety. How many times have you checked you have your ticket or e-ticket on your mobile, your passport if you are travelling abroad, your money, or directions to your destination? The list of checking opportunities is endless if you choose to make it so.

This obsessive checking allows your Gremlin to morph into anxious, obsessive Gremlin, constantly reminding you to check again and again!

Travel can take you out of your comfort zone. Your comfort zone is a behavioural space where your activities and behaviours fit a routine and pattern that minimises stress and risk. It provides a state of mental security. Your Gremlin will benefit in obvious ways: regular happiness, low anxiety, and reduced stress.

Everyone's comfort zone is different, and what may expand your horizons may paralyse someone else.

When you travel, you have to adapt to new people, expectations, cultural practices, accent or language, food and much more – and that is just in your own homeland!

Some people love this challenge to expand their horizons and absorb the situation with grace and humour. This confidence diffuses embarrassment and enables all people involved to cooperate, to create a solution or positive experience. You project a confident and relaxed aura and your Gremlin behaves accordingly.

Other people feel anxious and nervous when they are out of their comfort zone resulting in petulance, grumpiness and ill humour.

* Walmsley E J Stickgold R (2011) Sleep Med Clin. 6(1): 97–108. Memory, Sleep and Dreaming: Experiencing Consolidation

Arriving at your destination, you may be overawed by the architecture, clothes, magnitude of the space, or the magnitude of the energy (e.g. Niagara Falls). On the other hand, you may be shocked by your hotel room or disappointed by the standard of the food. These emotions, compounded by a new place and the tiring experience of travelling, can be challenging, and exhausting, depleting your stock of positive emotions.

Of course, the opposite can be true with excitement, wonder and curiosity, creating enthusiasm and delight.

The answer for both you and your Gremlin is sleep. Sleep is a great restorer and leveller of emotions. It has the power to allow your body to regenerate its energy and recalibrate your emotional state.

Some studies suggest that the quantity and quality of sleep have a profound impact on learning and memory.*

Research suggests that sleep helps learning and memory in two distinct ways. Sleep enhances optimal attention when awake, improving efficient learning, and sleep itself has a role in the consolidation of memory, which is essential for learning new information. Scientists are currently exploring whether there is a relationship between the consolidation of different types of memories and the various stages of sleep.

Since travelling offers opportunities for learning and the creation of new memories, it is obvious that learning how to relax quickly and get the benefit of deep, restful sleep is a great life skill.

In Gremlin parlance, sleep restores your emotional balance.

When Commander Tim Peake returned to Earth after his amazing flight into space and residence in the International Space Station, one of the first things he indicated he wanted was to talk to his family, have a cold beer and a sleep.

Travel can be a great investment in yourself (and your Gremlin). You are exposed not only to new environments but also to new people, lifestyles and cultures. You may gain a new insight into your homeland or the world and some people find a fresh purpose in life. You may feel exhilarated, renewed and inspired, which are uplifting emotions for your Gremlin to ingest and for you to experience.

It must be said, however, that some people spend endless hours looking for a British fry-up or fish and chips and in doing so may miss some amazing local foods and opportunities. There is a saying that 'travel broadens the mind', however the mind needs to be open in the first place for this to happen.

Your Gremlin is always up for it but if you don't feed it enthusiastic emotions, it cannot respond by nurturing your feelings.

Travel can help you put life into perspective. Seeing other people cope or not cope provides an interesting opportunity to assess yourself. Regular travel, be it commuting, travelling by train, or flying to another part of the country or another continent, develops confidence and competence.

I love to watch people on the London Underground who regularly make a specific journey. They stride with confidence to the appropriate stairway and they know exactly where to stand on the platform for when the train door opens. Even better, they know which way to walk to find the exit on the way out!

Confidence makes you less anxious and when it comes to changes in your day-to-day life, people who regularly travel may show more confidence and be more open and willing to accept change.

**"The further you get away from yourself,
the more challenging it is.
Not to be in your comfort zone is great fun."
Benedict Cumberbatch**

We all have varied, different, and personal life experiences which affect our responses and therefore our emotions, and as a result, our Gremlin. Awareness of our responses – self-awareness – helps us to choose how we wish to react and how we wish to develop as an individual.

CHAPTER 11:

EXCESSIVE BEHAVIOURS AND THEIR EMOTIONS

The Diva

The origin of the word 'diva' is from the Latin feminine of dīvus or god – a female deity. In Italy, it referred to women of outstanding talent in the world of opera and the male equivalent (divo) was reserved for the most outstanding tenors.

In the twenty-first century, a diva can refer to a man or woman with a reputation for being temperamental or difficult to please. They're the type who must have their way exactly.

Such people are often rude and belittle others, believing that everyone is beneath them and that they are loved and adored by everyone. Thus, a diva is selfish, often spoilt, and overly dramatic. They are high maintenance, emotionally demanding, and they create unnecessary drama and fuss over their appearance.

The tabloids and social media are full of the diva antics of actors, singers and celebrities; their tantrums, emotional outbursts and posturing.

What emotions are they feeding their Gremlin and what sort of Gremlins are they creating in this emotional frenzy?

This behaviour has spread beyond 'celebrities' to Generations Y and Z, some of the parents and children of the twenty-first century. It is fuelled by soaps like *EastEnders*, *Hollyoaks*, *Emmerdale*, *The Only Way is Essex* and all the *Real Housewives of...* programmes. Excessive diva behaviours are the norm and are replayed on TVs, laptops, computers and tablets all over the house, country and world.

This has the effect of desensitising our emotions, resulting in acceptance of these excessive behaviours. You may then start to copy the behaviour and language and make it your own.

A great example of this is the word 'like', often used instead of a pause (posh description: linguistic filler). Its extensive use in Generation Z's language has been fuelled by its popularity with pop stars and other god-like figures of this generation.

When the Spice Girls released their song *Wannabe*, they epitomised a generation's demands of 'I want' and 'I must have'. Aspirations are good, motivational and energising, however 'wants' and 'must-haves' have resulted in huge credit card and mortgage debt as this emotional hijack has continued.

The UK used to be a conservative (note the small 'c') rational country, the results of two World Wars. But as great, great grandparents and great grandparents die, so has the 'spend within your limits' mindset.

With contactless debit and credit cards, spending happens on a whim and buying on the internet is addictive and exciting. (Guess what emotions your Gremlin is munching!)

Seventy-five per cent of everything bought in 2014 was paid for by card. Card spending accounted for 32% of GDP in the UK in 2014 and was critical for the economy. Card spending is expected to continue to grow over the next decade and to overtake cash as the predominant way to pay. (UK Cards Association)

The credit card bill may create some emotions of fear, dismay and guilt for shoppers but their Gremlin can always be assuaged by more spending or...a wake-up call. Creating a plan to pay off the debt and become more aware of spending habits is an option that will give their Gremlin far more comfort in the long term.

Keeping up with the diva images displayed in magazines, adverts, soaps and films becomes addictive. Most of us do this at some level or other and for a short time the emotions we feed our Gremlin are pleasure and happiness, but a few extra pounds around the waist will create annoyance, disgust and unhappiness if we get into the habit of comparing ourselves negatively with celebrity divas.

For some, an unfriendly word, look or comment can create emotions of despair and confusion; it conflicts with the diva image that the person is trying so desperately to project. When you feed these emotions to your Gremlin, it morphs into rejection, confusion and feelings of insecurity.

A 2016 NHS study has found 19.7% of women aged 16-24 screened positive for self-harm and 28.2% had a mental health condition. Some of these highly concerning figures may be related to the diva and his or her unreal expectations. Poor self-image and an insecure feeling that they are not living up to the 'prince' or 'princess' ideal that so many of their parents encouraged in their youth may also be a factor.

Diva behaviour reminds me of phone-mania! Today the phone is the latest must-have accessory. It must be held in the hand all the time!

Just walk along a busy street and watch how many people are engaged in texting/Facebook/Twitter/Instagram. It seems it is essential to tell everyone what you are doing, who you are doing it with and how.

I carried out some research with people over 18 and discovered that the main reasons for constant updates was (their words):

- Encouraging people to take notice of them
- Getting feedback on their activities
- Bragging
- Wanting to be noticed and liked while enjoying the moment
- Keeping up with others' activities
- Making memories to share

The emotions these people described were:

- Excitement
- Joy
- Annoyance
- Anticipation
- Anger
- Admiration
- Apprehension
- Surprise
- Distraction
- Thoughtfulness

That's quite a mixture of reactions to pass through their mobile device! They also described this constant updating as an opportunity to 'air brush' their life.

Their Gremlin was very busy reacting to many of these emotions and this behaviour could continue throughout their day and often well into the night. Poor Gremlin, it must be totally exhausted by all these emotions!

The conclusion is that regular, excessive, over-the-top diva behaviours are exhausting, resulting in reduced well-being and poor health. This is not a great future for our young people.

From an early age, most children in the twenty-first century are encouraged to 'know their rights', put themselves first and regularly take the role of prince or princess. This may encourage future generations of divas...who knows?

This type of behaviour can put a lot of pressure on shy, quiet children as well as extroverts, and as we have learned in this chapter, lots of pressure (real or perceived) causes strong emotions resulting in an unhealthy Gremlin in an unhealthy body.

This should be a wake-up call to everyone as pressures build in our consumer-led, must-have society. Stress could become rampant with increased mental health issues relating to obesity, diabetes, heart disease, cancer, stroke, lung and liver disease.

Isn't it time we ditched the diva behaviour and gave our Gremlins a rest?

CHAPTER 12:

GET YOUR MOJO BACK!

By now, you will appreciate how the way we think creates the emotions our Gremlin consumes and makes your Gremlin (and you) unwell, happy and healthy (full of MoJo), or somewhere in between.

The five diva behaviours – dissatisfied, displeased, discontented, disappointed, disgruntled – sum up what stress looks like emotionally, leading to unhappiness, physical and psychological ill health.

The antidote to diva behaviours, the five Cs:

- Control your emotions appropriately
- Choose your life experiences
- Commit to being the best you can be
- Confidence to trust and believe in yourself
- Challenge yourself and be true to your values

These five Cs provide a set of targets that support good health and happiness as well as reducing stress.

Life Skills

There are other life skills that can support good health, reduce stress and tension, and make MoJo! These are:

- Taking responsibility for your actions
- Being thoughtful and caring towards others
- Having a laugh and being humorous
- Learning to employ flexible thinking to create solutions
- Having an optimistic outlook on life
- Sharing time with family and friends
- Getting exercise and eating healthily

Lots of people control their emotions very tightly, smothering their Gremlin with internalised emotions. This will very quickly suffocate your Gremlin, creating significant physical and/or mental ill health (stress).

Your Gremlin also benefits from the right amount of pressure. Too little pressure in your life creates boredom, and a bored Gremlin will exhaust you and suck out every good emotion you have.

If you feed your Gremlin the emotions created from the right amount of pressure, it will enjoy emotions related to satisfaction, enjoyment, good challenge, fulfilment and pleasure. In other words, MoJo!

If you regularly feed your Gremlin too much pressure, it will feed on emotions of fear, anger, negativity, worry, low self-esteem or insomnia, and it will become exhausted. Stress in motion is a downward spiral towards physical and/or mental ill health.

It is therefore vital that you learn how to take stock of your life and attitude and change whatever needs to change, so you can regain a grounded personality which supports both you and your Gremlin.

There are many aspects of a grounded personality:

- Good self-esteem/confidence
- Patience
- Clear moral awareness
- Clear spiritual convictions
- Courage
- Respectful of yourself and others
- Stable
- Sincere
- Practical
- Flexible
- Optimistic
- Sense of humour

These innate values combine to create a calm yet vibrant person who feeds their Gremlin emotions which integrate powerfully, producing compassion, forgiveness, tolerance, contentment and self-discipline. MoJo Gremlin!

These are life-supporting emotions which enhance self-esteem, confidence, patience and self-awareness. Such skills are the basis of good health, and GREAT MoJo!

SUSTAIN YOUR MOJO!

www.healthgremlins.com is packed full of encouraging ideas to sustain that GREAT feeling – your MoJo. Ann's video is a good place to start as it shows how you can build up your motivation to start making some positive changes in your life.

So why not rock along to the site and make a commitment to yourself to try out some new approaches and discover what works for you?

And you're welcome to contact Ann to arrange a motivational presentation, training or personal coaching.

She can be contacted at ann@healthgremlins.com